WALKED HOME BY AN ANGEL

BY
FRED JERKINS JR
D. Min

FIRST EDITION

Walked Home By An Angel

DEDICATION

===============================

I dedicate this book, "Walked Home By An Angel," to a vast tapestry of individuals who have played pivotal roles in my life's journey. Firstly, to my beloved siblings, whose unwavering support and love have been the bedrock of my existence, shaping me into the person I am today.

To my cherished wife, Sylvia, who do boundless love, patience, and understanding have been my guiding light through life's trials and triumphs. To my children, Sharene, Sybil, Fred III, Rodney Roy, who have brought immeasurable joy and meaning into my world, inspiring me to persevere and strive for excellence in all endeavors.

To each grandchild and great-grandchild, whose laughter and innocence remind me of the beauty and purity of life. To my extended family, whose camaraderie and shared memories have enriched my life beyond measure.

To my friends, whose companionship and loyalty have provided solace and strength during times of adversity. To the parishioners of my church, whose faith and devotion has been a source of inspiration and encouragement throughout my spiritual journey.

Finally, to my spiritual sons and daughters, among who stands out: Lois McClam and Marlowe Self-Ford, a beacon of light and resilience amidst life's storms. Marlowe, you have mirrored my own experiences and encounters with angelic protection, reaffirming the profound presence of divine grace in our lives.

To each and every individual mentioned and to countless others unnamed, I offer this humble dedication as a token of gratitude for the indelible impact you have had on my life.

May this book serve as a testament to the power of faith, love, and the enduring presence of angels in our midst.

I dedicate this book.

CONTENT

Note: Walked Home by an Angel Foundation International

Introduction:

In the tapestry of human existence, the hand of the divine weaves intricate patterns of grace, redemption, and providence. Each thread tells a story—a narrative of faith, hope, and the unfathomable love that guides us along the winding paths of life's pilgrimage. "Walked Home By An Angel" is a true story and testament to these sacred encounters, where the ordinary meets the extraordinary, and the mundane becomes infused with the presence of the divine.

Within the pages of this book, we embark on a journey of spiritual exploration—a journey marked by moments of profound revelation, transformation, and divine intervention. Through the lens of Christian faith, we encounter stories that resonate with the timeless truths of Scripture, where angels serve as helpers and messengers of

God's mercy, compassion, and boundless love.

Drawing from the rich tapestry of biblical narratives and personal testimonies, "Walked Home By An Angel" invites readers to experience the power of divine providence in their own lives. From the whispered prayers of the faithful to the miraculous interventions that defy human comprehension, these stories illuminate the sacred intersections between heaven and earth, where the veil between the seen and unseen is momentarily lifted.

At its core, this book is a celebration of the extraordinary ways in which God's grace manifests in the midst of our everyday struggles and triumphs. It is a reminder that even in our darkest hours, we are never alone—that the hand of God is ever-present, guiding us with steadfast love and unwavering faithfulness.

As we journey together through the pages of "Walked Home By An Angel," may our hearts be opened to the wonder and mystery of God's providential care.

May we be inspired to seek the divine presence in every moment, trusting in the promise that angels walk among us, guiding us home to the embrace of our heavenly Father.

May this book serve as a source of comfort, inspiration, and spiritual nourishment—a reminder that in the journey of faith, we are surrounded by a cloud of witnesses, both seen and unseen, who accompany us on the path toward our eternal home.

Chapter 1:
Angels Are Real

Colossians 1:16 *"For by him (Jesus Christ) were all things created, that are in heaven, and that are in earth, visible and invisible, whether* they be *thrones, or dominions, or principalities, or powers: all things were created by him, and for him:"*

In the vast expanse of creation, angels stand as celestial beings, messengers of the Almighty, and guardians of His divine will. Their existence is not merely a matter of myth or legend but is firmly rooted in the sacred texts of the Bible, where their presence and significance are affirmed time and again.

4

Genesis 3:24
"God drove out the man, and at the east of the Garden of Eden he placed the cherubim and a flaming sword that turned every way to guard the way to the tree of life."

From the very beginning, angels are woven into the fabric of God's creation. In the Garden of Eden, cherubim are stationed to guard the entrance, signifying their role as protectors and custodians of God's holiness.

Genesis 22:11
"And the angel of the LORD called unto him out of heaven, and said, Abraham, Abraham: and he said, Here am I".

Genesis 32:1
"And Jacob went on his way, and the angels of God met him"

Exodus 23:20
"Behold, I send an Angel before thee, to keep thee in the way, and to bring thee into the place which I have prepared".

Psalm 91:11-12
"For he will command his angels concerning you to guard you in all your ways. On their hands, they will bear you up, lest you strike your foot against a stone."

The book of Exodus and the book of Psalms bear witness to the protective care of angels, emphasizing their role in safeguarding God's people from harm and danger, keeping them and bringing them to their final destination. Their presence is a constant source of reassurance and comfort to those who trust in the Lord.

Psalm 103: 20-21
"Bless the Lord, ye his angels, that excel in strength, that do his commandments, hearkening unto the voice of his word.²¹ Bless ye the Lord, all ye his hosts; ye ministers of his, that do his pleasure".

Angels do not make decisions on their own and they cannot be manipulated by humans, God's angels obey his commandments.

Psalm 104.4
"Who maketh (create) his angels spirits; his ministers a flaming fire:"

Zechariah 2:3
"And, behold, the angel that talked with me went forth, and another angel went out to meet him"

The angels of the Lord not only lead, guard, and protect God's children, but, sometimes when they are on their God given mission they will talk with God's children.

Daniel 6:22-23
"My God hath sent his angel, and hath shut the lions' mouths, that they have not hurt me: forasmuch as before him innocency was found in me; and also before thee, O king, have I done no hurt".

In the New Testament we find references of angels as announcers and messengers.

Luke 1:26-38
In the Gospel of Luke, we encounter the angel Gabriel, who announces the miraculous conception of Jesus to Mary. This divine encounter serves as a profound demonstration of God's sovereignty and the pivotal role angels play in the unfolding of His redemptive plan.

In the teachings of Jesus, we find references to angels as guardians of the innocent and advocates for the marginalized. Their presence underscores the importance of humility, faith, and purity of heart in the Kingdom of Heaven.

Matthew 28:1-7
"At that time the disciples came to Jesus, saying, 'Who is the greatest in the kingdom of heaven?' And calling to him a child, he put him in the midst of them and said, 'Truly, I say to you, unless you turn and become like children, you will never enter the kingdom of heaven. Whoever humbles himself like this child is the greatest in the kingdom of heaven. Whoever receives one such child in my name receives me, but whoever causes one of these little ones who believe in me to sin, it would be better for him to have a great millstone fastened around his neck and to be drowned in the depth of the sea."

Matthew 26:53
"Thinkest thou that I cannot now pray to my Father, and he shall presently give me more than twelve legions of angels?

Angels have the power and ability to rescue at God's command.

Matthew 28:2
"And, behold, there was a great earthquake: for the angel of the Lord descended from heaven, and came and rolled back the stone from the door, and sat upon it".

After the resurrection of Christ, "one angel" rolled the heavy stone away from the entrance of the tomb not to let Jesus out, but to allow his disciple to enter. Afterward the Angel sat upon the stone that he moved out of the way.

Acts 5:19-20
"But the angel of the Lord by night opened the prison doors, and brought them forth, and said, ²⁰ Go, stand and speak in the temple to the people all the words of this life.

Hebrews 1:14
"Are they not all ministering spirits, sent forth to minister for them who shall be heirs of salvation?"

Hebrews 12:22
"But ye are come unto mount Sion, and unto the city of the living God, the heavenly Jerusalem, and to an innumerable company of angels,"

Hebrews 13:2
"Do not neglect to show hospitality to strangers, for thereby some have entertained angels unawares."

The epistles of the New Testament remind us of the mysterious nature of angelic visitations. They often appear incognito, assuming human form, to fulfill God's purposes and bring blessings to His people.

Through these scriptural passages and countless others, the reality of angels emerges as a foundational truth of the Christian faith. They serve as messengers of God's love, instruments of His grace, and companions on our journey of faith. As we embark on this exploration of angelic encounters, may our hearts be opened to the wondrous mysteries of God's divine realm, and may we be ever mindful of the presence of angels in our midst.

Chapter 2:
Fallen Angels and Demons Are Real

In the fabric of spiritual existence, the reality of fallen angels and demons stands as a sobering reminder of the cosmic struggle between good and evil. While angels were created as holy beings to serve God's purposes, some chose to rebel against Him, resulting in their expulsion from heaven and descent into darkness.

Isaiah 14:12-15
"How you are fallen from heaven, O Day Star, son of Dawn! How you are cut down to the ground, you who laid the nations low!
You said in your heart, 'I will ascend to heaven; above the stars of God I will set my throne on high; I will sit on the mount of assembly in the far reaches of the north; I will ascend above the heights of the clouds; I will make myself like the Most High.'

But you are brought down to Sheol, to the far reaches of the pit."

The prophet Isaiah vividly portrays the fall of Lucifer, once a radiant angelic being, who sought to exalt himself above God and was cast down from heaven as a result of his rebellion.

Matthew 8:28-32
"And when he came to the other side, to the country of the Gadarenes, two demon-possessed men met him, coming out of the tombs, so fierce that no one could pass that way. And behold, they cried out, 'What have you to do with us, O Son of God? Have you come here to torment us before the time?' Now a herd of many pigs was feeding at some distance from them. Moreover, the demons begged him, saying,
'If you cast us out, send us away into the herd of pigs And he said to them, 'Go.'
So they came out and went into the pigs, and behold, the whole herd rushed down the steep bank into the sea and drowned in the waters."

In the Gospels, we witness Jesus' encounters with demons, demonstrating His authority over the powers of darkness. These encounters serve as a testament to the reality of spiritual oppression and the transformative power of Christ to deliver individuals from bondage and affliction.

Ephesians 6:12
"For we do not wrestle against flesh and blood, but against the rulers, against the authorities, against the cosmic powers over this present darkness, against the spiritual forces of evil in the heavenly places."

The apostle Paul underscores the reality of spiritual warfare, highlighting the existence of demonic entities that seek to oppose God's purposes and deceive humanity. The battle we face is not merely physical but spiritual, requiring spiritual armor and divine strength to stand firm against the schemes of the enemy.

Revelation 12:7-9

"Now war arose in heaven, Michael and his angels fighting against the dragon. And the dragon and his angels fought back, but he was defeated, and there was no longer any place for them in heaven. And the great dragon was thrown down, that ancient serpent, who is called the devil and Satan, the deceiver of the whole world—he was thrown down to the earth, and his angels were thrown down with him."

The book of Revelation provides further insight into the future cosmic conflict between the forces of light and darkness. Satan once a cherub of highest rank will again lead a rebellion against God but will ultimately be defeated and cast out of first and second heaven along with his cohorts.

As we navigate the complexities of spiritual warfare, let us heed the warnings of Scripture and remain vigilant against the schemes of the enemy. Through faith in Christ and the power of His name, we can overcome the forces of darkness and stand firm in the victory won for us on the cross. May we be strengthened by the truth of God's Word and empowered by the Holy Spirit to resist the temptations of the evil one and walk in the light of God's love and grace.

Chapter 3:
Demons Can Harass And Possess Humans

The existence of demonic harassment and possession is a reality affirmed throughout the pages of Scripture. While the concept may evoke fear and uncertainty, the Word of God offers insight into the nature of spiritual oppression and the means by which individuals can find deliverance and freedom.

Matthew 17:14-18
"And when they came to the crowd, a man came up to him and, kneeling before him, said, 'Lord, have mercy on my son, for he has seizures and he suffers terribly. For often he falls into the fire, and often into the water. And I brought him to your disciples, and they could not heal him.' And Jesus answered, 'O faithless and twisted generation, how long am I to be with you? How

long am I to bear with you? Bring him here to me.' And Jesus rebuked the demon, and it came out of him, and the boy was healed instantly."

In this passage, we witness Jesus' encounter with a boy who is tormented by a demon. The demon causes the boy to suffer greatly, manifesting in seizures and dangerous behavior. Jesus demonstrates His authority over the demonic realm by commanding the demon to leave, resulting in the boy's immediate healing.

Mark 5:1-15
"They came to the other side of the sea, to the country of the Gerasenes. And when Jesus had stepped out of the boat, immediately there met him out of the tombs a man with an unclean spirit. He lived among the tombs.

And no one could bind him anymore, not even with a chain, for he had often been bound with shackles and chains, but he wrenched the chains apart, and he broke the shackles in pieces. No one had the strength to subdue him. Night and day among the tombs and on the mountains he was always crying out and cutting himself with stones. And when he saw Jesus from afar, he ran and fell down before him. And crying out with a loud voice, he said, 'What have you to do with me, Jesus, Son of the Most High God? I adjure you by God, do not torment me.' For he was saying to him, 'Come out of the man, you unclean spirit!' And Jesus asked him, 'What is your name?' He replied, 'My name is Legion, for we are many.' And he begged him earnestly not to send them out of the country."

This account illustrates a man possessed by a legion of demons. The demons exert control over the man, causing him to engage in self-destructive behavior and live among the tombs. Jesus confronts the demons and commands them to leave, restoring the man to his right mind and freeing him from bondage.

Acts 16:16-18

"As we were going to the place of prayer, we were met by a slave girl who had a spirit of divination and brought her owners much gain by fortune-telling. She followed Paul and us, crying out, 'These men are servants of the Most High God, who proclaim to you the way of salvation.' And this she kept doing for many days. Paul, having become greatly annoyed, turned and said to the spirit, 'I command you in the name of Jesus Christ to come out of her.' And it came out that very hour."

In this passage, we encounter a girl possessed by a spirit of divination. The spirit enables her to predict the future, bringing profit to her owners.

Paul, filled with the Holy Spirit, commands the spirit to leave, demonstrating the authority believers possess in the name of Jesus Christ.

These Biblical accounts underscore the reality of demonic harassment and possession. While the manifestations may vary, the underlying truth remains constant: demonic forces seek to oppress, deceive, and destroy. Yet, through the power of Jesus Christ and the authority bestowed upon believers, individuals can find deliverance and freedom from the grip of darkness.

As we confront the realities of spiritual warfare, let us stand firm in the truth of God's Word, wielding the weapons of prayer, faith, and the name of Jesus Christ. May we be vigilant against the schemes of the enemy, trusting in the promise of God's protection and provision, and may we be instruments of His grace, bringing light into the darkest places and proclaiming freedom to the captives.

Chapter 4:
Witchcraft Workers Summon Demons To Harass Humans

Throughout Scripture, the practice of witchcraft and sorcery is condemned as an abomination before the Lord. Those who engage in such dark arts seek to manipulate spiritual forces for their own gain, often invoking demonic entities to carry out their nefarious purposes.

Deuteronomy 18:10-12
"There shall not be found among you anyone who burns his son or his daughter as an offering, anyone who practices divination or tells fortunes or interprets omens, or a sorcerer or a charmer or a medium or a necromancer or one who inquires of the dead, for whoever does these things is an abomination to the Lord. And because of these abominations the Lord your God is driving them out before you."

In this passage, the Lord warns His people against engaging in various forms of divination, sorcery, and necromancy. These practices are not only forbidden but are considered detestable in the sight of God.

1 Samuel 15:23
"For rebellion is as the sin of divination, and presumption is as iniquity and idolatry. Because you have rejected the word of the Lord, he has also rejected you from being king."

The prophet Samuel equates rebellion with the sin of divination, emphasizing the severity of engaging in practices that seek to circumvent God's authority and wisdom.

Acts 16:16-19

"As we were going to the place of prayer, we were met by a slave girl who had a spirit of divination and brought her owners much gain by fortune-telling. She followed Paul and us, crying out, 'These men are servants of the Most High God, who proclaim to you the way of salvation.' And this she kept doing for many days. Paul, having become greatly annoyed, turned and said to the spirit, 'I command you in the name of Jesus Christ to come out of her.' And it came out that very hour. But when her owners saw that their hope of gain was gone, they seized Paul and Silas and dragged them into the marketplace before the rulers."

This narrative from the book of Acts illustrates the connection between witchcraft and demonic influence. The slave girl possessed by a spirit of divination brings profit to her owners through fortune-telling. Paul, empowered by the Holy Spirit, commands the spirit to leave, resulting in the disruption of the witchcraft workers' schemes.

Ephesians 6:12
"For we do not wrestle against flesh and blood, but against the rulers, against the authorities, against the cosmic powers over this present darkness, against the spiritual forces of evil in the heavenly places."

The apostle Paul reminds believers that our battle is not against mere human adversaries but against spiritual forces of evil. Witchcraft and sorcery are conduits through which demonic entities seek to exert their influence and disrupt God's purposes.

As followers of Christ, we are called to stand firm against the powers of darkness, resisting the allure of witchcraft and sorcery. Through prayer, obedience to God's Word, and reliance on the Holy Spirit, we can overcome the schemes of the enemy and walk in the light of God's truth and righteousness.

May we heed the warnings of Scripture and flee from all forms of darkness, trusting in the power of Jesus Christ to deliver us from evil and to guide us in the paths of righteousness for His name's sake.

Chapter 5:
Demonic Activity in a Small Country Town

In the quaint and idyllic setting of South Jersey, a small country town nestled amidst verdant pastures and the tranquility of daily life was shattered by a sinister presence lurking in the shadows. What began as whispers and murmurs soon escalated into a crescendo of fear and uncertainty as reports of demonic activity spread like wildfire through the tight-knit community.

The Unexplained Phenomena

It started with subtle disturbances—a flickering of lights, inexplicable shadows darting across moonlit streets, and eerie whispers echoing through the stillness of the night. Residents spoke in hushed tones of strange occurrences: objects moving on their own accord, unsettling dreams plagued by sinister visions, and inexplicable bouts of illness afflicting both man and beast.

The Gathering Darkness

As the weeks passed, the atmosphere in South Jersey grew increasingly oppressive, weighed down by an unseen malevolence that seemed to permeate every corner of the town. Churchgoers whispered prayers of protection, seeking refuge in the sanctuary of faith, while others turned to superstition and folklore in a desperate bid to ward off the encroaching darkness.

A Call to Action

In the face of mounting uncertainty, Pastor Minus, the spiritual shepherd of a South Jersey flock, rallied his congregation to stand firm against the forces of evil that threatened to engulf their community. Armed with the sword of God's Word and fortified by the power of prayer, they embarked on a journey of spiritual warfare, determined to confront the darkness head-on.

The Battle Unfolds

Night after night, Pastor Minus and his band of faithful warriors gathered in fervent prayer, lifting their voices in defiance against the powers of darkness that sought to ensnare their town. They proclaimed the victory of Christ over every principality and power, invoking the name of Jesus as their mighty fortress and stronghold.

Victory in the Midst of Darkness

Slowly but surely, the tide began to turn. As the prayers of the righteous ascended like incense before the throne of heaven, the oppressive grip of darkness loosened its hold on the South Jersey Country town. Demonic manifestations waned, replaced by an atmosphere of peace and renewed hope as the light of God's truth pierced through the veil of despair.

The Promise of Redemption

In the aftermath of the spiritual battle, the town's people emerged stronger and more united than ever before. Though scars of the ordeal remained, they served as a poignant reminder of the reality of spiritual warfare and the unwavering faithfulness of God in the face of adversity.

As the sun set on the small town, casting its golden glow upon the tranquil landscape, the townsfolk found solace in the promise of redemption and the eternal victory secured through Christ's triumph over sin and death.

In the annals of this town's history, the tale of demonic activity would be recounted for generations to come—a testament to the power of faith, the resilience of the human spirit, and the unshakeable truth that even in the darkest of nights, the light of God's love shines brightest.

Chapter 6:
Demons Using People for Evil Purposes

As the veil of darkness lifted from this town, revealing glimpses of light and hope, a sobering reality emerged—a reality that spoke of demons using individuals as vessels for malevolent purposes. In the aftermath of the spiritual warfare that gripped the small country town, stories began to surface of individuals ensnared in the clutches of demonic influence, their lives manipulated and distorted by forces beyond their control.

The Temptation of Power

There were some individuals, who resided in this town, who were seduced by promises of power and prestige, only to find themselves ensnared in a web of deception spun by demonic forces. Some sought solace in forbidden knowledge and occult practices, believing themselves masters of their own destiny, unaware of the insidious influence that lurked beneath the surface.

The Deception of Desperation

For others, desperation became the breeding ground for demonic manipulation. In the wake of hardship and loss, vulnerable souls found themselves susceptible to the whispered lies of the enemy, lured by false promises of relief and escape. The pursuit of quick fixes and easy solutions led them down a path of darkness, where the price of momentary reprieve came at a steep and devastating cost.

The Struggle for Liberation

In the midst of the town's turmoil, Pastor Minus and his congregation confronted the harsh reality of demonic seduction and manipulation with unwavering resolve. They bore witness to the anguish of those ensnared by the enemy's grasp, offering prayers of deliverance and compassion to those in need. With each intercession, they waged war against the principalities and powers that sought to destroy lives and sow seeds of discord within their community.

The Power of Redemption

Amidst the darkness that threatened to engulf the town folks, glimmers of hope emerged—testimonies of lives transformed by the redeeming power of Christ's love. Through the ministry of Pastor Minus and the fervent prayers of the faithful, individuals once bound by chains of darkness found freedom and restoration in the arms of their Savior. The light of God's truth pierced through the shadows, illuminating pathways of healing and reconciliation for those who dared to believe.

A Call to Vigilance

As the people of the town sought to rebuild and heal in the aftermath of its spiritual battle, Pastor Minus issued a solemn call to vigilance—a reminder that the struggle against demonic influence was ongoing and that the enemy remained ever vigilant in his quest to deceive and destroy. Through steadfast faith, prayer, and community support, they resolved to stand guard against the schemes of the enemy, knowing that in Christ, they possessed the ultimate victory over the forces of darkness.

The Triumph of Light Over Darkness

In the quiet moments that followed, the people of this small town bore witness to the transformative power of God's grace—a power that transcended the darkness and ushered in a new dawn of hope and redemption. Though the scars of spiritual warfare remained etched upon the landscape of their town, they served as a testament to the resilience of the human spirit and the unwavering faithfulness of a God who never abandoned His children in their hour of need.

As the town folks looked to the future with renewed faith and determination, they did so with the assurance that even in the darkest of nights, the light of God's love would shine brightly, guiding them on the path of righteousness and peace.

Chapter 7:
Demonic Activity Re-started and Increased

In the serene small town of South Jersey, where the rhythm of life flowed gently for a while, like a winding stream, an ominous darkness descended, heralding the resurgence of demonic activity that sent ripples of fear throughout the community. What had once been sporadic encounters with the supernatural now escalated into a torrent of malevolent manifestations, testing the faith and resolve of the residents like never before.

A Haunting Return

The resurgence of demonic activity caught the residents by surprise, like a sudden storm on a tranquil afternoon. What had seemed like isolated incidents now became a haunting presence, lingering in the shadows and casting a pall of unease over the once-peaceful town. Whispers of inexplicable phenomena spread like wildfire, leaving no corner untouched by the specter of fear.

Frequency of Malevolent Manifestations

The manifestations of evil spirits became more frequent, occurring with alarming regularity that left the residents on edge once again. Strange noises echoed through the night, chilling the hearts of those who dared to listen. Shadows danced menacingly in the moonlight, and unsettling dreams plagued the sleep of even the most devout believers. It was as though a veil of darkness had descended upon their town, threatening to engulf it in an abyss of fear and despair.

During the year of 1949, In the eerie stillness of the night, a sense of dread descended as a monstrous "bird like" creature with wings that spanned about a quarter of a mile, slowly glided across the darkened sky. The sound of its slowly flapping wings which were heard afar, grew louder and louder as it flew toward the town, the deafening noise echoing through the streets and rousing the town's residents from their slumber. As the monstrous creature approached their community, fear gripped their hearts with icy tendrils, sending shivers down their spines.

Huddled together in their beds, the children of South Jersey (including me) trembled with fear as the deafening noise of the_creature's flapping wings reverberated through the night air.

I can still recall the fear that gripped me as I watched my father rise from his bed, his voice filled with uncertainty as he muttered repeatedly, "What is it?"

As the menacing creature traversed the heavens, its ominous presence cast a pall over the town, shrouding it in a cloak of darkness and uncertainty.

The sheer magnitude of the creature's size struck terror into the hearts of all who beheld it, rendering even the bravest among them paralyzed with fear. Men and fathers dared not venture outside, and many refrained from so much as peeking out of their windows for fear of what they might see.

Only a few brave souls (including my father) dared to step outside and confront the terrifying spectacle that had unfolded in the night. With trembling hands and hearts pounding with fear, they gazed skyward and beheld the monstrous "bird like" creature with wings that seemed to stretch to the very edges of the horizon. The deafening roar of its wings filled the air, drowning out all other sound and leaving the residents of that town in a state of shock and disbelief. The monstrous bird slowly flew out of sight and the horrifying noise dissipated, but that sound, that noise yet lingers in my mind until today.

In the aftermath of the creature's ominous visitation, a sense of unease settled over the town like a thick fog, casting a shadow of fear over its inhabitants. Children cowered indoors, afraid to venture outside to play or attend school, while parents whispered anxiously amongst themselves, searching for answers to the inexplicable phenomenon that had gripped them that night. And as night fell once more, the memory of the monstrous creature lingered in the minds of all who had witnessed its terrifying presence, a chilling reminder of the dark forces that lurked beyond the realm of the known.

In the days that followed, a veil of silence descended upon the town, as if the residents sought to erase the horrifying experience from their collective memory. Most refused to speak of the monstrous creature that had cast a shadow of fear over their once peaceful community, as though they wished to "un-hear what they heard" the deafening noise that had shattered the tranquility of their lives. Yet, despite their best efforts to forget, the memory of that fateful night lingered in the minds of all who had witnessed it.

A Community in Turmoil

As the frequency of demonic activity increased, the townsfolk found themselves thrust into a state of turmoil. Some began to question the very foundations of their faith. The once-thriving community became a shadow of its former self, its streets deserted, and its spirit broken by the relentless onslaught of evil.

It was about 1951, Under the warm embrace of a spring sunny evening, the quaint streets of this small Southern New Jersey town were seemingly alive again, with the laughter and play of children.

It was around 4:30 p.m., a time when the day still held onto its brightness, the flowers were in full bloom, and the air was filled with the fresh scent of new beginnings.

On this particular evening, the children of the town were making the most of the beautiful weather, running around in their yards, riding bikes, and playing games that only required their imagination. Among these children was our family of siblings, we were known in the neighborhood for our close-knit bond and adventurous spirits.

As the sun began its slow descent in the sky, painting everything in a golden hue, something extraordinary happened. Without warning, we were stopped in our tracks, our games forgotten. Above us, in the clear blue sky, appeared a second sun. This celestial anomaly was just as large as the daily sun that we were accustomed to, but it was a reddish-orange color, glowing warmly but without the blinding beams of light that usually accompanied their familiar star. This second sun was lower in the sky, moving slowly from the south towards the north, traveling in a downward arc but never quite touching the earth.

We were awestruck by the sight. I was always keen to capture moments with my little camera, scrambled to take a photo. But in my excitement and nervousness, I fumbled, and the camera slipped from my grasp, clattering to the ground as the film spilled out, unexposed and ruined.

My siblings and I stood together, rooted to the spot in amazement, watching as the second large sun seemed to descend toward the earth. It moved slowly, majestically, as if bidding its time, before finally, it drifted out of sight, leaving behind a sky that once again belonged solely to the familiar sun.

This event as well as the monstrous creature that flew over our town two years earlier, marked a turning point for the small community. Whispers of the second sun spread like wildfire, with each retelling growing more fantastical.

We siblings, with our vivid imaginations, were the primary witnesses to this celestial phenomenon, and our account of the event stirred a mixture of awe, skepticism, and fear among the townsfolk.

It was evident that something extraordinary had occurred, something that defied explanation. This incident opened the door to a world of possibilities that many had never dared to consider. Supernatural occurrences, once the stuff of legend and lore, were now being whispered about with renewed fervor. The appearance of the second sun was not just a singular event; it was a harbinger of things to come, signaling an increase in supernatural activities on a level that the small town had never before witnessed.

As the days passed, the memory of the second sun lingered in the minds of the townspeople. For us children, it was a moment of pure wonder, a story that we would recount for years to come. For the adults, it was a reminder that the world was full of mysteries, some beautiful, some terrifying, but all demanding to be acknowledged.

In this small town, life eventually continued as it always had, but beneath the surface, a sense of anticipation hummed.

The community, once so sure of its place in the world, now found itself on the brink of something vast and unexplored. The second sun had opened their eyes, and there was no going back.

A Test of Faith

In the face of escalating darkness, Pastor Minus, the spiritual leader, again stood as a beacon of hope amidst the storm. With unwavering faith and a heart burdened for his flock, he called upon his congregation again to stand firm against the powers of darkness that sought to overwhelm their town. Together, they lifted their voices in fervent prayer, seeking solace and strength in the promise of God's protection and deliverance.

A Renewed Resolve

Though the night seemed long and the shadows deep, the people refused to surrender to despair. Strengthened by their faith and united in purpose, they stood together in defiance against the forces of darkness, determined to reclaim their town from the clutches of evil. With each passing day, their resolve grew stronger, fueled by the unwavering belief that the light of God's love would ultimately prevail over the darkness that threatened to consume them.

The Promise of Redemption

As dawn broke over this small town, casting its golden light upon the seemingly tranquil landscape. All though it was months later after the gigantic flying creature phenomenon, and the second sun phenomenon, finally a sense of hope dawned in the hearts of its residents. Though the battle against darkness was far from over, they bounced back and found comfort in the knowledge that they were not alone.

With faith as their shield and prayer as their weapon, they embraced the promise of redemption, trusting in the power of God's love to banish the shadows and usher in a new dawn of peace and restoration.

Chapter 8:
A Mom Who Was a Woman of Faith

In the heart of the 1940s and 1950s, amidst the trials and triumphs of life, there stood a beacon of strength, grace, and unwavering faith—there was my mother. She was a woman whose life was guided by the timeless truths of the Holy Scriptures, a testament to the power of God's love and the transformative impact of a life lived in service to Him.

Roots of Faith

Born into a world fraught with adversity and inequality, my mother's journey was one marked by resilience and unwavering faith. From a young age, she was instilled with the values of compassion, integrity, and humility—qualities that would shape her character and define her legacy as a woman of God.

A Life of Devotion

As a devoted wife and mother, my mom poured her heart and soul into nurturing her family with love and wisdom drawn from the pages of the Bible. In the sacred teachings of scripture, she found solace, strength, and guidance for every aspect of life—from the joys of motherhood to the challenges of daily living in a world rife with injustice and uncertainty.

A Model of Virtue

My mother embodied the virtues of faith, hope, and perseverance in the face of adversity. She stood as a living testament to the transformative power of God's grace, inspiring all who knew her to walk in the footsteps of righteousness and compassion.

Guiding light through her unwavering commitment to God's word, my mother became a guiding light in our home and community—a source of comfort, counsel, and unwavering support for those in need. Her prayers were a lifeline in times of trouble, her words a balm to wounded hearts, and her love a reflection of the boundless grace of our Heavenly Father.

Legacy of Love

As her children, we were blessed to witness the depth of my mother's faith and the impact of her steadfast devotion to God. She taught us to seek first the kingdom of heaven, to love our neighbors as ourselves, and to walk in the footsteps of Jesus with humility and grace.

An Enduring Influence

Though she has since passed into glory, my mother's legacy lives on in the lives of all who knew her—a testament to the enduring power of faith, hope, and love. Her memory is etched upon our hearts, a beacon of light that continues to guide us through life's trials and triumphs, reminding us always of the profound impact of a life lived in service to God.

In Remembrance

In the quiet moments of reflection, I am reminded of the countless sacrifices my mother made, the countless prayers she offered, and the countless lives she touched with her unwavering faith and unconditional love. She was more than a woman of faith; she was a living example of God's grace, a testament to the transformative power of His love, and a cherished beacon of light in a world that often feels shrouded in darkness.

As I hold her memory close within my heart, I am overwhelmed with thankfulness for the invaluable treasure of her existence—a treasure that perpetually motivates and elevates those fortunate enough to have crossed paths with her.

My mother transcended mere faith; she personified divine love, exemplifying God's unwavering devotion and serving as a cherished testament to the transformative influence of a life dedicated to Him.

Chapter 9:
A Mom Who Reared Her Children in the Fear and Admonition of the Lord

In the heart of the 1950s, amidst the backdrop of racial injustice and social upheaval, my mother stood as a steadfast beacon of faith, raising her children in the fear and admonition of the Lord, much like Lois and Eunice from the Book of Timothy in the Bible. Her unwavering commitment to instilling the values of righteousness and obedience to God's commandments shaped our upbringing and set the foundation for a life rooted in faith and virtue.

The Ten Commandments

From an early age, my mother taught us the sacredness of God's commandments, impressing upon us the importance of honoring our father and mother, respecting the sanctity of life, and upholding the principles of honesty and integrity in all our dealings. Through her gentle guidance and unwavering example, she instilled within us a reverence for God's law and a deep-seated understanding of the moral principles it espoused.

The Difference Between Light and Darkness

As we grew older, my mother lovingly explained to us the stark contrast between the teachings of Jesus Christ and the deceitful ways of Satan. She emphasized the importance of discerning truth from falsehood, right from wrong, light from darkness, and righteousness from sin.

Through her teachings, we learned to embrace the light of Christ and reject the temptations of the evil one, walking steadfastly in the path of righteousness and grace.

Salvation and Redemption

My mother's greatest desire was for her children to experience the transformative power of salvation through faith in Jesus Christ. With tender love and unwavering conviction, she shared the gospel message with us, explaining the profound significance of Christ's sacrifice on the cross and the hope of redemption available to all who believe. Through her guidance, we came to understand the depth of God's love and the eternal promise of salvation that awaits those who place their trust in Him.

Heaven, Hell, and the Reality of Spiritual Warfare

With gentle yet unwavering resolve, my mother taught us about the realities of heaven and hell, the eternal consequences of our choices, and the existence of spiritual demonic warfare that rages unseen in the heavenly realms. She impressed upon us the urgency of living a life dedicated to God's purposes, knowing that our eternal destiny hung in the balance. Through her teachings, we learned to stand firm against witchcraft and all the schemes of the enemy, armed with the armor of God and the assurance of His protection.

Avoidance of Witchcraft and Deception

In a world filled with deception and spiritual darkness, my mother repeatedly cautioned us against the allure of witchcraft and the deceptive practices of the occult.

With wisdom and discernment, she taught us to reject the empty promises of worldly pursuits and to cling steadfastly to the truth of God's Word in the Holy Scripture.

Through her guidance and example, we learned to discern good from evil, light from darkness, and to walk in the ways of righteousness, even in the face of adversity.

In the nurturing embrace of my mother's love and guidance, we grew to understand the profound importance of living a life surrendered to God's will, grounded in His truth, and steadfast in faith.

Her unwavering commitment to rearing us in the fear and admonition of the Lord left an indelible mark on our hearts, shaping our character, strengthening our faith, and instilling within us a deep-seated reverence for God and His eternal purposes.

Chapter 10:
A Mom's Prayers Remembered

Amidst the trials and triumphs of life, my mother's prayers echoed like a sacred melody, weaving a tapestry of faith, hope, and divine protection over our family. Each day, she lifted her voice to heaven, seeking God's provision and angelic protection for her loved ones, both at home and away. Her prayers were a testament to her unwavering trust in God's faithfulness and the profound depth of her love for us.

From the humble confines of our home, my mother often knelt in prayer, her heart pouring out its deepest longings to the God who hears and answers the cries of His children. With every petition, she entrusted our family into the loving arms of our Heavenly Father, seeking His guidance, provision, and divine protection in the midst of life's uncertainties.

Divine Provision

In a world marked by scarcity and adversity, as children who grew up poor, my mother's prayers were a lifeline of hope, trusting in God's promise to provide for our every need according to His riches in glory. Through seasons of plenty and seasons of want, she stood unwavering in her faith, believing that God's provision would sustain us and carry us through even the darkest of times.

Angelic Protection

As a mother, mom's greatest fear was the safety and well-being of her family, both at home and afar. With fervent devotion, she invoked the presence of God's angels to encamp around us, shielding us from harm and danger, and guiding our steps along paths of righteousness and peace.

Her prayers were a fortress of protection, a tangible expression of her boundless love and concern for our welfare.

A Legacy of Faith

As her children, we were the beneficiaries of mom's unwavering faith and steadfast prayers. We witnessed firsthand the miraculous provision of God and the divine protection that surrounded our lives like a shield. Through her example, we learned the power of prayer, the importance of trust in God's promises, and the enduring legacy of a life surrendered to His will.

A Mother's Love Endures

Though the years have passed, the memory of my mother's prayers remains etched upon my heart—a sacred reminder of her unwavering love and devotion to her family. Her prayers were a lifeline in times of trouble, a source of comfort in moments of despair, and a beacon of hope that illuminated our path through life's darkest valleys.

In Remembrance

As I reflect on the legacy of my mother's prayers, I am filled with gratitude for the profound impact of her faith on our lives. Her prayers were not merely words spoken into the void but a powerful testament to the transformative power of God's love and the enduring strength of a mother's devotion.

As the years pass and memories fade, I am comforted by the knowledge that my mother's prayers continue to reverberate throughout eternity, a sacred offering of love and faithfulness that transcends time and space.

In her prayers, I find solace, strength, and the abiding assurance that God's love endures forever, guiding us through life's trials and triumphs with grace and mercy beyond measure.

Chapter 11:
Demonic Activity Hit Our Family

In the early 1950s, our family consisted of our mom and dad, and seven children, five sons who were born first and two daughters. I yet remember how we faced harrowing encounters with demonic activity that shook the very foundation of our faith and tested our resolve in ways we never imagined.

Ghostly Encounter on the Road

One ominous night, as my parents drove home along a desolate road, a chilling presence enveloped our car, bringing it to an abrupt halt. Panic surged through my parents' veins as they attempted to restart the engine, but to no avail. With trembling hands, my father lifted the hood, revealing a haunting sight—a white, ghostly figure materialized before him, its spectral form hovering ominously. With a fervent prayer, my father and mother watched in awe as the ghostly figure ascended into the night sky, releasing its grip on our car and allowing it to re-start, allowing them to continue their journey home. The encounter left an indelible mark on our family, a stark reminder of the spiritual forces at play in the unseen realm.

True Boy's Mysterious Fate

Our beloved family pet dog, True Boy, was a faithful companion who roamed the wooded paths near our home with boundless energy and enthusiasm. One fateful day, he returned home distressed, his eyes filled with fear and his tail tucked between his legs. True Boy attempted to lead three of my siblings, including myself, down the familiar wooded path, as if to warn us of impending danger lurking within.

Yet, instinctively, we resisted his urging, sensing the ominous presence that loomed ahead. Two days later, True Boy was found lifeless in the woods, his once vibrant spirit extinguished by an unseen malevolence that haunted our family's every step.

Curtis's Fateful Encounter With Witchcraft

As the eldest brother, Curtis at the age of fourteen, ventured into the perilous depths of the night, his path intersected with a woman ensnared by the dark arts of witchcraft. Ignoring our mother's warnings, Curtis found himself ensnared in a web of temptation and deceit, as the woman sought to lure him into the abyss of her sinister desires. With steadfast resolve, Curtis rebuffed her advances, fleeing into the night as the shadows whispered sinister secrets and unseen forces pursued his every step flattening the tall bushes along the roadside. Only the flattened bushes along the roadside and a weird noise of wind, bore witness to the unseen presence that trailed beside him as he ran as fast as he could towards home, a chilling reminder of the darkness that lurked in the shadows.

Mentally Disturbed People Roaming The Streets

In addition to the unsettling encounters with the demonic forces that seemed to linger within the fabric of our family's history, there existed another eerie phenomenon just thirty miles west of our town. There, nestled amidst the trees and shadows, stood a well-known mental institution. While such places were meant to provide care and solace to those afflicted with various mental illnesses, this institution harbored its own sinister secrets.

Occasionally, the tranquility of our town would be shattered by the escape of some of the institution's patients.

These troubled souls would find their way into our midst, seeking refuge amidst the cover of the woods or even wandering the streets, lost in their own torment. It was a sight both pitiful and chilling to behold.

These escapees were not merely struggling with mental disturbances; some seemed to be vessels for darker forces. They would emit strange noises, reminiscent of wild animals, their growls echoing through the night. Passersby were often startled and frightened by their presence, their minds unable to comprehend the depths of the madness that gripped these unfortunate souls.

At times, their desperation would drive them to break into the homes of our townsfolk, seeking sustenance in stolen morsels of food. It was as if their afflictions and the darkness that plagued them knew no bounds, spilling over into our once peaceful community.

The fear that gripped our town now had new dimensions. It wasn't just the whispers of witchcraft manifestations or the shadowy specters of our own familial past that haunted us; it was the very real threat posed by these tormented individuals, both human and something beyond human comprehension.

As the nights grew longer and the shadows deeper, the townsfolk found themselves perpetually on edge, wary of the unseen forces that lurked in the darkness. Each rustle of leaves, each howl of wind, seemed to carry with it the echoes of a deeper, more primal fear—a fear of the unknown, of the darkness that dwelled within and without.

And so, we lived our lives, ever vigilant, ever wary, knowing that in the quiet of the night, anything could happen, and that the line between the rational and the irrational, the sane and the mad, was thinner than we dared to admit.

A Family's Resilience in the Face of Darkness

Though the specter of demonic activity cast a shadow over our family, we refused to be consumed by fear and despair. Through fervent prayer and unwavering faith, we confronted the forces of darkness with the light of God's truth, knowing that His divine protection would shield us from harm. Each encounter strengthened our resolve and deepened our reliance on the power of God's love to overcome even the greatest of adversities.

In the midst of spiritual darkness, our family stood united, anchored by the unwavering belief that God's grace would lead us through the darkest of nights and into the dawn of a new day. Though the shadows may loom large, the light of His love shines brighter still, illuminating our path with hope, courage, and unwavering faith. Through every trial and tribulation, we clung to the promise that no darkness could withstand the radiant brilliance of God's eternal light.

Chapter 12:
Walked Home By An Angel

It was yet 1950s, in this town where fear and uncertainty lurked in the shadows, my brother Lee, and I found ourselves navigating the darkness of a world tainted by demonic presence. With the recent harrowing experiences of our family fresh in our minds, and knowing about the mentally disturbed patients who roamed our streets, we embarked on a journey that would forever alter our perception of divine protection and heavenly intervention.

A Mother's Prayer

As the sun dipped below the horizon, casting long shadows across the dusty dirt road, our mom entrusted us with a sacred mission—to fetch groceries from the old country store a mile and a half away. With a note clutched in

Lee's hand and just enough money to pay for each item, our mom's prayers enveloped us in a cloak of divine protection as we set out into the night.

The Purchased Groceries, Journey Home Into Darkness

The air hung heavy with the weight of impending darkness as Lee and I stepped out of the old country store, Lee's arms laden with bags of groceries and our minds swirling with apprehension. The sun had long since dipped below the horizon, leaving behind a world cloaked in shadow and uncertainty. As we ventured into the night, the eerie stillness of the countryside enveloped us, punctuated only by the distant chirping of crickets and the faint glow of lamplight from scattered homes in the distance.

With trepidation in our hearts and fear of the unknown gnawing at our souls, Lee and I trudged along the dimly lit road, our eyes darting nervously to the wooded areas that flanked our path. The memory of our family's recent encounters with demonic forces loomed large in our minds, fueling our anxiety and compelling us to walk down the middle of the road, far from the menacing shadows that threatened to ensnare us. With each step we took, a sense of foreboding settled over us like a suffocating shroud.

As we walked, the darkness seemed to close in around us, the only illumination provided by the faint glow of distant lamplights and the twinkling stars overhead. Every rustle of the leaves and whisper of the wind sent shivers down our spines, our imaginations running wild with visions of unseen terrors lurking in the shadows.

A Glimmer of Hope

However, amid the darkness, a glimmer of hope pierced through the gloom—a silent reassurance that we were not alone. With each step, Lee and I felt the warmth of our mother's prayers encircle us like a protective cloak, guiding us through the labyrinthine paths of uncertainty and fear.

Encounter With the Unknown

As we approached the crest of a hill, shrouded in darkness and uncertainty, a towering "man like" figure materialized before us, its massive form casting an imposing shadow across the road. Lee and my initial terror gave way to desperate cries for answers, as we demanded to know the identity of the mysterious figure. Yet, the giant remained silent, its back turned to us as it led the way towards our home.

Divine Protection Unveiled

With each step we took, our fear began to dissipate, replaced by a sense of awe and wonder at the realization that a celestial guardian was guiding us. The giant figure walked ahead of us, a silent sentinel against the forces of darkness that lurked in the shadows. As we finally reached the safety of our home, the figure paused in the middle of the road, its presence a tangible reminder of God's promise to protect His children from harm.

A Revelation of Faith

As we watched in awe from the safety of our doorstep, Lee and I bore witness to the miraculous disappearance of the giant figure of a man, its ethereal form fading into the night like a whisper on the wind. In that moment, we knew without a doubt that we had been *"Walked Home By An Angel"*—a divine encounter that affirmed our faith and renewed our trust in the protective power of God's heavenly hosts.

As we stepped into the warmth and safety of our home, Lee and I shared our miraculous encounter with our family, our hearts overflowing with gratitude and joy.

Though the darkness of the night had threatened to engulf us, and though we did not know what lurked in the woods, we emerged unscathed, guided by the unseen hand of divine providence. In the quiet moments that followed, we offered prayers of thanks and praise, knowing that we had been enveloped in the protective embrace of God's love—an experience that would forever be etched into the tapestry of our faith journey. We had been *"Walked Home By An Angel"*.

Chapter 13:
Walked Home By An Angel - A Memorable Experience

In that quiet town of South Jersey, where the echoes of fear and uncertainty reverberated through the streets, the memory of divine intervention yet lingers in our hearts and minds. Our encounter with an angelic presence, amidst the backdrop of pervasive demonic activity and our family's own brush with the supernatural, had left an indelible mark on our souls—a testament to the unwavering protection and providence of a God who watches over His children with boundless love and grace.

A Testimony of Divine Protection

As Lee and I recount our remarkable journey, of how we were *Walked Home By An Angel,* everyone who we told our story to, listened with rapt attention, their hearts stirred by our testimony of God's miraculous intervention in the face of darkness and despair. With each retelling, the memory of that fateful night came flooding back, vivid and alive in our minds—the towering figure that had emerged from the shadows, the palpable sense of peace that had enveloped us, and the unmistakable presence of divine protection that had guided us safely home.

A Beacon of Hope

In this town, which was gripped by fear and uncertainty, our story, served as a beacon of hope—a reminder that even in the darkest of times, God's light shines brightest. our testimony of angelic protection resonated deeply with the fellow townsfolk, offering solace and reassurance in the face of the unknown.

For in our story, they found a glimmer of hope amidst the shadows—a reminder that no matter how dire the circumstances may seem, we are never truly alone.

A Testament to Faith

As we share our story far and wide, Lee and I bear witness to the transformative power of faith and the enduring strength of God's love. Our encounter with an angelic presence has reaffirmed our belief in the Supernatural and deepened our trust in the providence of a God who works all things for the good of those who love Him. Through our testimony, we are inspiring others to trust in God's promises, to live by faith not by fear and to hold fast to the hope that He brings in the midst of life's trials and tribulations.

A Legacy of Gratitude

Though time passed and seasons changed, the memory of our divine encounter remained etched in the fabric of our lives—a treasured reminder of God's faithfulness and the profound impact of

His angelic protection. As we looked back on that fateful night, Lee and I are filled with gratitude for the gift of divine intervention that had guided us safely home. Our story has become a cherished part of our family's legacy, a testament to the power of prayer and the enduring presence of God's angels in our lives.

As Lee and I continued to share our story with others, we do so with hearts overflowing with gratitude and awe at the miraculous ways in which God had worked in our lives. Our encounter with an angelic presence has become a source of inspiration and encouragement to all who hear it, reminding them of the boundless love and protection that God offers to His children.

And, though the memory of that night would fade with time, the impact of God's divine intervention would endure forever—a timeless reminder of the extraordinary ways in which He watches over His beloved children with unwavering care and compassion.

Chapter 14:
Lessons Learned from Supernatural Angelic Encounters

Since the first remarkable encounter with what I can only describe as a celestial being, my life has been filled with experiences that both defy conventional understanding and reinforce the belief in a protective, divine presence. These encounters have ranged from profound dreams and visions in the still of the night to comforting whispers in moments of peril to Supernatural Angelic interventions and appearances, guiding me through life's tumultuous journey. The lessons I've gleaned from these angelic interactions have shaped my understanding of the world, spirituality, and the protective embrace of unseen forces.

Lesson 1: The Protective Veil of the Divine

One of the earliest and most profound lessons imparted to me was the realization that we are never truly alone. The encounters taught me that angels, divine messengers of God; watch over us, providing a protective veil. They have revealed dangers lurking in the shadows, both physical and spiritual, and have offered guidance on how to navigate these perils, ensuring my safety and that of my family.

Lesson 2: Discerning Spirits

Through these encounters, I've learned the importance of discernment. Many times, Angels have revealed the true intentions of those around me, distinguishing between those who mean well and those harboring ill intentions.

This discernment has been a guiding light, helping me navigate complex social landscapes and protect myself from potential harm.

Lesson 3: Heeding Divine Warnings

A pivotal lesson has been the importance of heeding divine warnings. These messages, often conveyed through dreams, visions, angelic appearances or a still small voice have included precise instructions on how to avoid imminent dangers. By following these directives, I've been able to avert situations that could have led to harm, affirming the benevolent watchfulness of these celestial guides.

Lesson 4: The Power of Prayer

A recurring theme in my experiences has been the power of prayer. I've learned that through prayer, we can call upon God to send his angels to surround and protect us from seen and unseen dangers. This realization has transformed my daily prayers into powerful decrees for divine protection, covering not just for myself but also for my loved ones. I have a special prayer that I pray to God every day when I leave home and when I returned home. When I go for a walk, or when I get in my car to go for a drive or when I'm riding with someone else, my daily prayer is this: "Lord Jesus, please send your Angels of protection and surround me with angelic protection, keep me safe from seen and un-seen dangers and, keep my immediate family and loves ones safe, Amen". I pray this prayer every day, and you should too. I have learned not to take life for granted.

Lesson 5: Overflowing Blessings

Among the most uplifting lessons has been the assurance of God's blessings.

Angels have conveyed messages of hope and affirmation, reminding me that divine favor is not just a concept but a tangible reality. These messages have often been specific, detailing the blessings awaiting me and my family, encouraging us to remain patient and steadfast in faith.

Lesson 6: The Unseen Battle

My angelic encounters have also revealed the ongoing spiritual battle for our souls. This knowledge has instilled in me a deeper appreciation for the guardianship angels provide, standing at the front lines of this battle, shielding us from spiritual harm and guiding us towards light and truth.

Conclusion: A Life Transformed

Since my first encounter, my life has been irrevocably transformed. The knowledge that God's angels are always watching, ready to offer protection, guidance, and divine messages to his children, this has instilled in me an unshakeable faith. My daily prayer is a testament to this transformation, a plea for protection, and recognition of the powerful allies we have in the celestial realm.

The lessons learned from these supernatural angelic encounters have not only enriched my spiritual life but have also offered a blueprint for navigating the physical world. They serve as a constant reminder that behind the veil of our reality lies a divine order, a network of celestial beings dedicated to our protection and spiritual growth.

In sharing these lessons, my hope is that others may find comfort, guidance, and the reassurance that we are never alone in our journey through life. The Angels, God's messengers, are always with God's children, offering their protection, wisdom and love.

Chapter 15:
Lessons Learned from Demonic Encounters

Throughout my spiritual journey, I have encountered forces of darkness just as I have been guided by the light of angelic beings. These encounters with the demonic have been challenging, yet they have imparted crucial lessons about the spiritual realm, the power of faith, and the protection afforded by divine forces. In this chapter, I will share the insights gained from these encounters and the Biblical principles that have guided me through them.

The Relative Power of Demons and Angels

One of the most comforting revelations from my experiences has been the understanding that demons, whether they manifest in visible forms or remain unseen, do not possess the same level of power as God's angels. This realization aligns with the scriptural affirmation that *"He who is in you is greater than he who is in the world"* (*1 John 4:4*). In every encounter, the presence and intervention of God's angels have demonstrated that divine power far surpasses any malevolent force.

The Magnetism of the Occult

Through personal experiences and observation, I've learned that certain objects and practices associated with witchcraft and the occult can attract demonic entities to one's space. Items such as good luck charms, four-leaf clovers, elephant statues with trunks facing upward, snake rings, crystal balls, Ouija boards, and tarot cards, along with practices like séances and ceremonies intended to contact the dead, have served as conduits for demonic influence.

Moreover, engaging in immoral behavior, abusing mind-altering substances, and excessively focusing on the devil and demonic activity rather than on God's redemptive plan can also draw these malevolent spirits closer.

This insight has underscored the importance of guarding one's environment and mind from influences that can open doors to darkness.

The Power of Deliverance

One of the most profound lessons has been witnessing the power of God to deliver individuals from depression, obsession, and possession by demonic entities. These experiences have affirmed that no one is beyond the reach of God's saving grace and supernatural intervention. Deliverance has often come through prayer, fasting, and the casting out of demons by the invocation of Jesus' name, emphasizing that true power and liberation lie in divine authority.

The Dangers of Misplaced Remedies

In seeking protection or deliverance from demonic influences, I learned that resorting to objects or practices of witchcraft for help only exacerbates the problem. This misguided approach can strengthen the grip of these entities rather than warding them off. The biblical account of the church in Ephesus, where new believers burned their scrolls of magic as a public act of turning away from darkness to light (*Acts 19:19*), serves as a powerful example of renouncing occult ties and embracing spiritual purity.

The First Steps to Freedom

The initial step in breaking free from demonic influences involves the physical removal and destruction of any objects linked to witchcraft or the occult.

This act of renunciation not only symbolizes but also enacts a break from the powers of darkness, paving the way for God's light to enter and cleanse.

Spiritual Resistance

Echoing the scriptural directive, "Resist the devil, and he will flee from you" (James 4:7), my encounters have taught me the importance of spiritual resistance.

This resistance is not passive but active, involving prayer, the reading and proclamation of Scripture, and the reaffirmation of one's faith in Christ. It's through these spiritual disciplines that one can maintain a posture of defiance against demonic forces.

Conclusion

The lessons learned from demonic encounters have been invaluable in my spiritual growth and understanding of the spiritual warfare that believers are called to engage in. By recognizing the signs of demonic influence, asserting the authority given through Christ, and adhering to biblical principles of spiritual warfare, believers can navigate through these challenges with the assurance of victory in Jesus Christ. There are many believers because of their faith, that have received total deliverance from demonic depression and obsession.

Chapter 16:
Angelic Intervention Number One

Many years have passed since my first encounter with angelic presence, yet the memory remains as vivid as ever. It's a testament to the enduring power of faith and the miraculous interventions that can unfold in our lives.

At the tender age of sixteen, in the bustling city of Atlantic City, New Jersey, I found myself standing in front of a small storefront Christian church. It was there, in the warmth of the congregation's embrace, that I first encountered Jesus Christ as my personal Savior and was filled with the Holy Spirit. The moment was transformative, setting me on a path illuminated by divine purpose.

By the time I turned seventeen, I could feel the weight of God's calling upon my life. It was unmistakable, a gentle but insistent tug at the core of my being. And so, with trembling yet resolute steps, I answered that call to preach the Gospel.

It was a calling that led me to street corners and alleyways, where the echoes of sin were loudest, and souls hungered for redemption.

"One such street corner, at the intersection of Massachusetts Avenue and Melrose in Atlantic City, New Jersey, became the setting for my first street corner revival. There was a bar on the adjacent corner. It was open 24 hours and known for the violent situations that took place there. My first encounter with Angelic protection occurred since my salvation experience was on that corner.

The air crackled with anticipation as I lifted my voice to proclaim the Word of God. But amidst the fervor of preaching, a discordant note pierced the night – the anguished cries of a woman possessed by demonic forces.

Her presence was a stark reminder of the spiritual battle raging unseen around us. Yet, anchored in the authority of Christ, I refused to be deterred. With unwavering faith, I confronted the darkness that sought to disrupt the divine message. Turning to face the woman, I felt a surge of divine power coursing through me. With a voice tempered by the Spirit's authority, I commanded, 'In the name of Jesus Christ,' the demonic presence to be silent. And in a moment of awe-inspiring obedience, the woman's torment ceased, her mouth sealed shut until the message had been delivered in its entirety. I believe that God had an Angel there on that street corner protecting me as I preached the gospel. Months later, that bar shut down indefinitely."

It was a demonstration of God's sovereignty over the forces of darkness, a tangible manifestation of His power to deliver and redeem. In the aftermath of that encounter, as souls responded to the call of salvation, I stood in prayer beside the woman once tormented by demons. Many on that day were liberated by the grace of God.

But this was just the beginning – a precursor to the multiple angelic encounters that would punctuate my journey of faith. From those whispered assurances in moments of doubt to unseen hands guiding my steps, the presence of angels became woven into the fabric of my life.

Each encounter served as a reminder of God's unfailing love and His promise to never leave nor forsake His children. And as I reflect on the journey that brought me to this moment, I am filled with gratitude for the angels both seen and unseen who have walked alongside me, guiding me ever closer to the heart of God's purpose for my life.

Chapter 17:
Angelic Intervention Number Two

The year was 1964, and at twenty-one years old, I found myself navigating the twists and turns of life with a newfound sense of responsibility. Married to a beautiful, devout woman, our journey together was just beginning, marked by faith and the promise of a shared future.

In those early days of marriage, we resided in a modest apartment nestled in the heart of Atlantic City, New Jersey. My days were filled with hard work as a member of the labor union, Local 272, where I labored in construction to provide for my growing family. Despite the challenges, the pay was sufficient, affording us the opportunity to upgrade to a larger, more comfortable apartment on Adam's Avenue in Pleasantville, New Jersey.

It was a day like any other as I prepared to leave our apartment and make my way towards New Road on Woodland Avenue, little did I know, it would mark a pivotal moment a testament to the divine protection that encircled our lives.

As I merged onto the road, the mundane rhythm of daily life was shattered by a sudden jolt. In an instant, my car skidded, its wheels losing traction on the sandy surface. Panic surged through me as I realized the gravity of the situation – I was careening towards the intersection, the traffic on New Road flowing steadily in both directions.

In that heart-stopping moment, when disaster seemed inevitable, something extraordinary occurred. Miraculously, inexplicably, my car veered to the right, gliding along the shoulder of the road with a precision that defied logic.

It was as though unseen hands had guided the steering wheel, steering me away from the path of imminent danger.

In the aftermath of the near-miss, a profound sense of awe and gratitude washed over me. I knew, without a shadow of a doubt, that I had been the recipient of divine intervention. It was a stark reminder of God's providence and the unfailing presence of His angels, ever watchful, ever vigilant.

As I reflected on the events of that fateful day, I was struck by the realization that God's protection had not been confined to the spiritual realm alone. His love extended to the tangible, mundane aspects of life even the simple act of driving down a road.

It was a sobering reminder to heed His admonition to be vigilant, to drive safely, and to approach each moment with a reverence for the precious gift of life. And yet, intertwined with that cautionary tale was a profound sense of reassurance – the knowledge that, no matter the trials we may face, we are never alone.

For on that day, amidst the chaos of a busy intersection, I had been enveloped in the comforting embrace of angelic protection. As the days passed, the clarity of that moment would soften in my mind, yet the enduring essence of God's vigilant presence would forever be engraved upon the canvas of my heart.

Chapter 18:
Angelic Intervention Number Three

In the year 1966, we were now living in a new apartment in Atlantic City, NJ. Our lives were filled with the joy and wonder that comes with parenthood. Our first daughter, Sharene, was about fifteen months old, her laughter and boundless energy bringing light into our home. Yet, amidst the hustle and bustle of daily life, a moment of divine intervention would unfold, revealing the miraculous protection of angelic beings.

It was a Friday night, and my wife and I had made plans to attend a gospel singing program in Mizpah, New Jersey. Sharene, our precious little girl, had already been tucked into bed, her angelic face peaceful in slumber. As young, innocent parents, we assumed she would sleep soundly through the night, unaware of the danger that lurked in our absence.

With a sense of anticipation, we set out for the gospel program, eager to partake in the fellowship and praise. The atmosphere was electric, the music stirring our souls as we sat together on a pew, immersed in the joy of worship Yet, amidst the harmonies and melodies, a different kind of vision began to unfold before my eyes.

In an instant, I was transported from the sanctuary to the confines of our home, where Sharene lay sleeping in her bed. But as I watched, a sense of unease crept over me, for I saw her stir, her tiny form rising from the safety of her bed. In the dim light of the room, she wandered through the house, her cries of confusion echoing off the walls.

With a jolt, I was brought back to the reality of the gospel program, my heart pounding with a sense of urgency. Turning to my wife,

I shared the vision that had gripped me, the fear for our daughter's safety gnawing at my soul. Without hesitation, we made the decision to leave, our hearts racing as we raced back home.

The journey felt interminable, each passing moment filled with a sense of dread. Yet, as we finally pulled into the driveway, a wave of relief washed over me. Stepping into the house, Sharene was lying on the stair steps, her tear-stained face a stark reminder of the danger she had faced in our absence.

In that moment, I knew without a doubt that we had been granted divine protection, a guardian angel watching over our precious daughter until we could return to her side. It was a humbling reminder of God's unfailing love and His commitment to the safety and well-being of His children.

As we held Sharene in our arms, comforting her and soothing her tears, I couldn't help but marvel at the intricate ways in which God works His miracles. From the quiet whisper of a guardian angel to the vivid clarity of a vision, His presence was unmistakable, guiding us through the darkness and leading us safely home. As time progressed, the recollection of that night would inevitably diminish, yet the awareness of angelic guardianship would persist, forever Imprinted within our hearts.

Chapter 19:
Angelic Intervention Number Four

I believe that it was the year of 1970, and the road stretched out before us like a ribbon of promise, leading us towards our destination. My wife and I, accompanied by our young baby son Fred III, embarked on a journey eastward along the Black Horse Pike, Route 442. Little did we know, this seemingly ordinary drive would soon become a testament to the miraculous protection of angelic beings.

Behind the wheel of our brand-new Wild Cat Buick, resplendent in its red and black splendor, I felt a surge of pride and gratitude for the blessings bestowed upon us. As we sped towards our destination, the landscape blurred in our peripheral vision, the hum of the engine a steady rhythm beneath us.

But amidst the rush of the wind and the roar of the engine, a sudden shift in the atmosphere seized our attention. Up ahead, no more than four to six car lengths away, chaos erupted as a vehicle slammed on its brakes, its tires screeching in protest. Another car, heedless of the danger, had careened into its path, forcing a sudden and treacherous halt.

With reflexes honed by years of driving, I slammed on the brakes, our car lurching forward in a desperate attempt to avoid collision. But it was futile – the laws of physics and momentum conspired against us, threatening to hurl us into the heart of the impending disaster.

In that moment of terror, when death seemed imminent, something extraordinary occurred.

A force, unseen and incomprehensible, lifted our car from the asphalt as though it were weightless, guiding it with gentle precision towards the safety of the median island. It was a supernatural intervention, a divine hand reaching down from the heavens to protect us from harm.

As our car came to rest in the middle of the island, facing westward instead of continuing its eastward trajectory, a hush descended over us. The chaos of the highway faded into the background, replaced by a profound sense of awe and gratitude.

In the aftermath of the near miss, my wife and I exchanged incredulous glances, our hearts overflowing with thanksgiving. It was clear to us that we had been the recipients of divine intervention, the hand of God guiding us through the perilous waters of danger.

But it wasn't just the miraculous relocation of our car that left us in awe – it was the small yet unmistakable details that revealed the presence of angelic beings. Our gearshift, once firmly in drive, had been mysteriously shifted into park, ensuring our safety and bringing our car to a standstill.

As we sat in the quiet aftermath of the ordeal, our son Fred III nestled safely between us, I offered up a prayer of thanks to God for the angels who had watched over us that day. Their presence, though unseen, had been palpable, guiding our steps and protecting us from harm.

In the years that followed, the memory of that fateful day would serve as a constant reminder of the miraculous ways in which God works His wonders. And while the specifics may blur with the passage of time, the reality of divine intervention will forever be Inscribed in our hearts.

Chapter 20:
Angelic Intervention Number
Five

The year was 1975, our family, consisted of my wife and I along with our three children, had established a tradition of taking a family vacation twice a year. Sometimes we ventured to Maryland, occasionally to Florida, but our favorite destination was Springfield, Massachusetts. It held a special place in our hearts because my mother's. "baby sister' Catherine and her husband resided there. The bond with our aunt and uncle was profound, prompting frequent visits, especially since the drive from our home to their home was only about five hours.

On a particularly sunny morning, we eagerly packed our suitcases into the car, anticipating the adventures awaiting us. Before embarking on our journey, we paused to offer a prayer to God, seeking angelic protection during our travels. With hearts full of hope and excitement, we set off on our familiar route.

Our journey commenced on the NJ State Parkway, heading Northward. We then took the New Jersey Turnpike to New York. After Passing over the George Washington Bridge, and through the Lincoln tunnel to New York, we got on I-91. This highway would take us toward Connecticut and eventually to Springfield, Massachusetts. The initial leg of the drive proved to be pleasant; traffic was light, and the atmosphere in the car brimmed with joy.

In hindsight, I recall Just as we emerged from the tunnel's embrace; a flash of red caught my eye. Glancing to my side, I saw a sleek, brand-new Cadillac cruising along beside us. Its vibrant red paint glistened in the sunlight, and its polished exterior seemed to mirror the excitement bubbling within me.

For a moment, I was taken aback. What were the odds of encountering another traveler in such a picturesque manner? But as I looked closer, I noticed the occupants of the Cadillac—a family, just like ours, embarking on their own adventure.

A sense of camaraderie washed over me as we exchanged waves and smiles with the occupants of the red Cadillac. There was an unspoken understanding between us, a shared recognition of the joy that comes with embarking on a journey, whether it be towards a vacation spot or an unknown destination.

As we continued down Highway I-91, periodically passing each other with cheerful gestures, I couldn't help but feel grateful for this unexpected connection. In that moment, it was as if our paths had converged not by chance, but by some higher design—a reminder that even in the vastness of the world, we are all interconnected, bound together by the shared experience of life's adventures.

The encounter with the red Cadillac became a cherished memory, a symbol of the serendipitous moments that pepper our lives and remind us of the beauty that surrounds us, if only we take the time to notice. And as we drove on, the memory of that fleeting encounter lingered, a testament to the miracle that awaits us when we open our hearts to the unexpected.

After driving for about three hours, I was filled with a contagious energy, making the journey an enjoyable experience for the entire family. With the tank brimming with gas, I felt confident we would reach Springfield without any hiccups, with just an hour and a half of driving left. However, amidst the laughter and chatter, I began to experience something unusual.

A soft, yet distinct voice seemed to whisper in my ear, urging me to pull over at the next rest stop and get some rest. At first, I dismissed it, convinced that I was not tired. Yet, the voice persisted, repeating the same command with unwavering insistence.

Conflicted, I silently pondered my options. Despite my initial resistance, I could not shake off the feeling that there was a reason behind the mysterious voice's insistence. Finally, I relented, deciding to heed the advice and pull over at the upcoming rest stop.

As the family vehicle came to a halt, I could not help but feel a sense of unease mingled with curiosity. What was it that compelled me to stop, even though I felt wide-awake? With a sigh, I turned to my family, explaining my decision to take a short break.

Little did I know, this seemingly mundane choice would soon prove to be a pivotal moment in our journey—a moment where angelic protection would manifest once again, guiding us through unforeseen challenges.

As we resumed our journey after the rest stop, we felt refreshed and rejuvenated, unaware of the impending danger lurking ahead. Little did we know, the decision to pause had spared us from a catastrophe of unimaginable proportions.

Approaching the scene of an accident, the air became heavy with tension. The highway, once bustling with traffic, now resembled a scene from a nightmare. A ten to twelve car pileup sprawled across both lanes, a twisted maze of metal and debris.

Mangled, bloody bodies were scattered all over the highway. Among the wreckage lay the red Cadillac, its once gleaming exterior now battered and broken, with the driver and his family trapped inside. It was a horrifying sight to behold.

The gravity of the situation hit me like a ton of bricks, my heart sinking as I realized the magnitude of the disaster. The air was thick with the stench of burning rubber and the smell of gasoline. Among the twisted metal, I could hear the groaning of agony echoed in my ears. In that moment, time seemed to stand still as I grappled with the sheer horror of what lay before me.

Emergency responders swarmed the area, their urgent movements a stark contrast to the eerie stillness of the wrecked vehicles. The flashing lights of police cars and ambulances painted a vivid tableau of chaos and despair. I could not shake the feeling of dread as I surveyed the scene, thankful beyond words that my family had been spared from such devastation.

Hours passed as we waited for the wreckage to be cleared, the weight of the tragedy hanging heavy in the air. Many lives had been lost that day, and we as a family could not help but feel a profound sense of gratitude for our own safety. We exchanged glances, our eyes filled with unspoken emotion as we silently thanked God for the unseen intervention of an Angel that had guided us to safety.

Eventually, the road was cleared, and we continued our journey with heavy hearts. The image of the accident would linger in our minds for days to come, a sobering reminder of the fragility of life. As I drove on, I could not help but marvel at the mysterious workings of fate, grateful for the still small voice that warned me to pull over at the next rest stop.

Chapter 21:
Arrival At The Vacation Destination

After enduring the harrowing ordeal of being delayed for hours on highway I-91, due to the tragic car pile-up, our family finally arrived at our destination in Springfield, Massachusetts. Relief flooded our hearts as we pulled into my aunt's driveway, grateful for our safe arrival yet heavy-hearted for the families who were not as fortunate.

Our aunt and uncle greeted us warmly as we stepped out of the car, our faces mirroring a mix of concern and relief. After unloading our luggage and settling in, we gathered in the cozy living room, seeking solace in each other's company.

As we recounted the events that led to our delay, a somber mood settled over the room. The realization of how narrowly we had escaped disaster weighed heavily on our minds, overshadowing the excitement of our vacation.

Amidst our conversation, Aunt Catherine reached for the remote and switched on the TV to catch up on the latest news. The screen flickered to life, and the news anchor's voice filled the room, reporting on the tragic accident that had caused our delay.

Our family watched in silence as the details unfolded before us. The accident, caused by a tractor-trailer suddenly jackknifing, sent shivers down our spines. We listened intently as the reporter confirmed the devastating toll the accident had taken, with many lives lost in the wreckage.

As the gravity of the situation sank in, a wave of solemnity washed over the room. We exchanged glances, our hearts heavy with empathy for the victims and their families. Though grateful for our own safety, we could not help but feel a profound sadness for those who weren't as fortunate.

In that moment, amidst the comfort of family and the safety of our vacation home, we held onto each other a little tighter, reminded once again of the fragility of life and the importance of cherishing every moment together.

Chapter 22:
The Journey Back Home

As the days of our vacation in Springfield, Massachusetts ended, we as a family found ourselves packing our belongings and preparing for the journey back to our home in Pomona, New Jersey. The memories of the tragic accident we had encountered on our way to Springfield still lingered in our minds, but we placed our trust in the Lord for protection as we embarked on the road once again.

After loading our car with luggage and offering a heartfelt prayer for angelic protection, we gathered with our relatives for one last time. Hugs were exchanged, tears were shed, and final goodbyes were said, each moment filled with a bittersweet mix of gratitude and anticipation.

Despite my lingering dread of the road ahead, I summoned the courage to start the journey back home, my faith unwavering in God's watchful care. With each mile we traveled, we leaned on our prayers for strength and protection, trusting that unseen hands guided us.

Five hours later, we finally pulled into our driveway in Pomona, New Jersey, greeted by the familiar sights and sounds of home. Relief washed over us as we realized we had safely completed our journey, a testament to the power of faith and divine protection.

With grateful hearts, we stepped out of our car into our home and gathered, in our living room. We bowed our heads in prayer once more, offering thanks and praise to the Lord for his unwavering love and protection throughout our travels.

As we embraced each other in a tight-knit circle, a sense of peace settled over us, knowing that we had been guided safely home. With hearts full of gratitude and faith renewed, we were inside our home, ready to cherish the memories of our vacation and the blessings of our journey for years to come.

Chapter 23:
Prayer and Caution in Seeking Angelic Protection

As we settled back into the comforts of our home, our hearts filled with gratitude for our safe return. We felt compelled to share a crucial piece of advice with others regarding the practice of praying for angelic protection.

While prayer is a powerful tool for spiritual connection and guidance, we emphasize the importance of caution and discernment, particularly when it comes to seeking the assistance of angels. We know all too well the dangers of straying into the realm of witchcraft or attempting to manipulate divine beings for selfish gain.

"It is vital," we caution, "to never worship angels *(Colossians 2:18)* or pray directly to angels or seek to manipulate their service for our own desires. Such actions are not only misguided but can lead down a path of darkness and deception."

Instead, we emphasize the necessity of directing prayers to God alone, trusting in His wisdom and sovereignty to dispatch His angels according to His divine will. "Prayers for angelic assistance, "must always be in alignment with God's will, purposes and intentions, never driven by selfish motives or desires."

Scripture assures us that whatever we ask in the name of Jesus Christ, according to His will, will be done. This promise underscores the importance of praying in alignment with God's purposes and desires.

When we pray for angelic assistance, we do so within the framework of God's will, trusting that He will send His angels to aid us in accordance with His divine plan.

It's crucial to remember that we should never pray to angels themselves or seek to manipulate them for our own selfish desires.

Again, such prayers veer into the realm of witchcraft and are contrary to God's will. Instead, we direct our prayers to God, asking Him to dispatch His angels to assist us in specific situations and endeavors.

We urged others to remember the words of Jesus himself, who taught us to pray "*Our Father, who art in heaven, hallowed be thy name,*" In these words, you acknowledged God's holiness and sovereignty over all creation. You must understand the importance of starting your prayers by praising God for His greatness and glory.

"*Thy kingdom come, thy will be done, on earth as it is in heaven,*" This line reminds you to align your desires with God's perfect will. You must understand, that praying for angelic protection means surrendering to God's plan and trusting that His purposes would prevail.

125

"Give us this day our daily bread," this line, recognizes your dependence on God for sustenance and provision. In seeking angelic assistance, you acknowledged your need for divine intervention in your daily life.

"And forgive us our trespasses, as we forgive those who trespass against us," you must also understand that harboring unforgiveness could hinder your prayers and disrupt their connection with God and His angels.

"Lead us not into temptation, but deliver us from evil," plead, seeking God's guidance and protection from the forces of darkness.

You must also know that praying for angelic assistance is also a prayer for spiritual warfare, trusting that God's angels would fight on your behalf against unseen enemies.

"For thine is the kingdom, the power, and the glory, forever and ever. Amen."

We conclude, affirming your faith in God's eternal sovereignty and authority You know that our prayers for angelic protection were heard and shall be answered by the Almighty, who reigns over all things.

As we shared our advice with others, we emphasized the importance of maintaining a pure and sincere heart in all spiritual practices. We encouraged others to seek angelic protection through prayers grounded in faith and trust, knowing that God's angels stand ready to assist those who walk in obedience to His will.

In conclusion, we reminded everyone whom we spoke too, to approach prayer with caution and discernment, never veering into practices that may lead astray from the true path of faith. "Let us seek the guidance and protection of God's angels," we urged," with hearts pure and intentions aligned with His perfect will."

Chapter 24:
Walked Home By An Angel Spiritually

In the sacred pages of the King James Bible, we find the timeless truths that illuminate the spiritual journey of every born-again believer. Just as Lee and I were guided home by an angelic presence, so too are you born again children of God, are accompanied by the indwelling Spirit of God, and surrounded by his heavenly hosts, as you navigate the trials and tribulations of life on your journey towards eternal glory.

The Journey of Faith

As believers, we are called to walk by faith, guided by the Word of God and empowered by the Holy Spirit who dwells within us. In *2 Corinthians 5:7*, we are reminded, *"For we walk by faith, not by sight."* Through faith, we are able to trust in the promises of

God and follow His leading, even when the path before us is shrouded in darkness.

The Indwelling Spirit

The Holy Spirit, who takes up residence within the hearts of believers, serves as our constant companion and guide. In *1 Corinthians 6:19*, we are told, *"What? Know ye not that your body is the temple of the Holy Ghost, which is in you, which ye have of God, and ye are not your own?"*

Through His presence, we are empowered to walk in obedience and righteousness, overcoming the temptations of the flesh and the schemes of the enemy.

Angelic Assistance

Although we have the Holy Spirit, God's angels, who serve as ministering spirits, are sent forth to minister to the heirs of salvation *(Hebrews 1:14)*, are at our disposal to assist us in our spiritual journey.

In *Psalm 91:11*, we are assured, *"For he shall give his angels charge over thee, to keep thee in all thy ways."* With their assistance, we are shielded from harm, guided through the darkest valleys, and strengthened in times of weakness.

The Armor of God

As we walk the spiritual path, we are also instructed to put on the whole armor of God, as outlined in *Ephesians 6:10-18*. This spiritual armor equips us to stand firm against the wiles of the devil and to withstand the fiery darts of the evil one. With the belt of truth, the breastplate of righteousness, the shield of faith, the helmet of salvation, and the sword of the Spirit, which is the word of God, we are prepared to wage spiritual warfare and emerge victorious in Christ.

The Promise of Glory

As we journey towards our heavenly home, we are filled with the hope and assurance of eternal glory. In *2 Corinthians 4:17-18*, we are reminded;

"For our light affliction, which is but for a moment, worketh for us a far more exceeding and eternal weight of glory; While we look not at the things which are seen, but at the things which are not seen: for the things which are seen are temporal; but the things which are not seen are eternal."

Through faith, we press onward, knowing that our present sufferings are but a prelude to the eternal glory that awaits us in the presence of our Savior.

Chapter 25: Conclusion

In the turbulent currents of our present era, we find ourselves amidst a tempest of global upheaval. Social and political unrest, racial tensions, and the alarming resurgence of anti-Semitism have cast a shadow over our world. In the midst of this chaos, a barrage of false ideologies, woke-ism, transgenderism, and the deceitful teachings of false prophets—that seek to distort truth and sow division among us, besieges us.

Many have strayed from their Biblical foundations, lured by the siren song of modern cancel culture, which silences dissent and enforce conformity with its intolerant dogmas.

Amidst this storm of confusion and despair, a profound sense of emptiness pervades the hearts of countless individuals, leading to an alarming escalation in suicide rates and a pervasive fear that grips our society. Violence and wickedness seem to lurk around every corner, while the scourge of human trafficking casts a long shadow over the most vulnerable among us.

Yet, in the midst of this blinding darkness, a beacon of hope shines forth—a light that pierces through the gloom and offers solace to the weary and downtrodden. It is the voice of Jesus Christ, calling out to all who are burdened and broken, offering rest and redemption to those who seek Him.

For Jesus Christ is the Light of the world, the one true source of hope and salvation in a world plagued by darkness.

In Him, we not only find the true light but, we find refuge from the storms that rage around us, and in His embrace, we discover the strength to endure.

He alone has the power to heal our wounds, to mend our brokenness, and to bring peace to our troubled hearts.

So let us heed the call of Jesus Christ and turn to Him in our hour of need. Let us cast aside the chains of fear and despair and take hold of the hope that He offers. For in Him, we find not only salvation, but also the promise of a brighter tomorrow—a tomorrow where the light of His love shines brightly dispelling the darkness and guiding us safely home.

Just as my brother Lee and I as youngsters found comfort and protection in the presence of an angel, so can you while travelling on this spiritual journey towards your heavenly home.

You too shall find solace in the promise of God's word, which assures us of His faithfulness and steadfast love. I believe that you as well as all of us children of God are being *walked home by an angel*. With each spiritual step we take, we draw closer to the day when we will stand in the presence of our Savior, surrounded by a great multitude of saints and angels, and hear the words of Jesus Christ say: *"Well done, thou good and faithful servant, enter into the joy of your Lord" (Matthew 25:21).*

Note:

Walked Home By an Angel Foundation International

The *Walked Home by an Angel* Foundation International is here! As we wrap up this shared story, let us talk about a big moment for me, the author. After telling real stories about our encounters with the supernatural and experiencing angelic protection, I decided to start this foundation. It is a nonprofit organization born from my own experiences and beliefs, offering hope and support in our big world.

Our foundation is all about bringing people together, no matter where they are from or what they believe. We believe everyone can find comfort and connection in our community, regardless of differences.

We are all about sharing—our stories, struggles, and especially our encounters with angels. We hold events in lots of different places, like homes, churches, schools, and hotels, where we can talk openly and support each other.

Our goal is to show how amazing it is when the extraordinary touches our everyday lives, especially when angels are involved. In addition, we are here to remind everyone that these Heavenly beings are real—they are messengers sent by God himself.

Let us share our stories with each other. There are those out there who will be strengthened spiritually and encouraged upon hearing your testimony.

If you are interested in sharing your story at one of our venues, you can contact us by email at: **WalkedHomebyanAngel@Gmail.com**

The translations referenced in this book have been selected to provide clarity and insight into the scriptures for a diverse audience.

1. King James Version (KJV)
2. New International Version (NIV)
3. English Standard Version (ESV)
4. New King James Version (NKJV)
5. New Living Translation (NLT)
6. Revised Standard Version (RSV)
7. The Message Bible (MSG)
8. Amplified Bible (AMP)
9. New American Standard Bible (NASB)
10. Christian Standard Bible (CSB)
11. Holman Christian Standard Bible (HCSB)
12. New Revised Standard Version (NRS)

Other books by the Author:

1. *The If's of God's Promised Blessing*
2. *The Last of the Last Days*
3. *Spouse Over the House or Mouse in the House*

All publications can be purchased from Amazon.com

Walked Home By An Angel

www.ingramcontent.com/pod-product-compliance
Lightning Source LLC
Chambersburg PA
CBHW072016040426
42447CB00009B/1648